The

Little Book

of

Romantic

Lies

By
BRUCE T. SMITH
&
LAURA GOECKE BURNS

CCC PUBLICATIONS

Published by

CCC Publications
1111 Rancho Conejo Blvd.
Suites 411 & 412
Newbury Park, CA 91320

Manufactured in the United States of America

Cover ©1997 CCC Publications

Cover/Interior production by Oasis Graphics

ISBN: 0-57644-042-7

If your local U.S. bookstore is out of stock, copies of this
book may be obtained by mailing check or money order for
$5.95 per book (plus $2.75 to cover postage and handling)
to:
CCC Publications; 111 Rancho Conejo Blvd.;
Suites 411 & 412; Newbury Park, CA 91320

Pre-publication Edition – 1/97

FOREWORD

Does SHE love me or does she not?
Is it ME he's interested in or just my........

In these times of uncertain relations
between men and women, half of the time,
no one "really" knows what the other
means — especially when it comes to
words of love and romance. So, to help
you in the game of love, we've written this
helpful book of translations. We suggest
you keep this book handy at all times... in
bars, at cocktail parties, and especially in
the bedroom!

<u>CONTENTS</u>

HIS LIES...

What He Says

* * *

What He REALLY Means!

You're a "10".

* * *

*You're a "4"
with a 6-pack.*

You mean everything
to me.

* * *

*Rich father,
hot Corvette,
sex....just not in
that order.*

I want to make love to you forever.

* * *

I can't wait to spend your inheritance.

I admire you
for being a
professional woman.

* * *

*That way, you can
support ME!*

I'm only 29!

* * *

*...months behind
in my
child support.*

I'm really into
oral sex.

* * *

*All I ever do is
TALK about it.*

I love you
for your mind.

* * *

*You're ugly as sin,
but you're
filthy rich.*

WOW!
You look great
first thing in
the morning.

* * *

*How about a quickie
before I throw
you out of my
apartment?*

You are my
one and only.

* * *

*For the next
10 minutes, anyway.*

I NEED you
by my side.

* * *

*I WANT you
underneath my belly.*

Baby, where have you
been all my life?

* * *

*Gee, I didn't notice
you lying underneath
the barstool !*

Sweetheart, things aren't always as they appear.

* * *

I have no idea how this g-string got caught in my zipper.

I want you
to marry me.

* * *

*I want your father
to hire me.*

Let's not think
about tomorrow.

* * *

*By then we'll
both be sober.*

Come on baby,
you'll love it.

* * *

I'll love it.
You'll feel like crap.

Let me prove my
love for you.

* * *

*Watch me take off
your bra with
my teeth.*

No, I don't mind
wearing a condom...

* * *

*...and from your looks,
I should probably
wear TWO.*

Would you like to come
up for a nightcap?

* * *

*No one EVER has sex
with me, SOBER.*

You're always in my
dreams.

* * *

*Especially when I
wet the bed.*

I've had a vasectomy.

* * *

...and I lied about my REAL name, too.

Looks aren't everything.

* * *

But don't expect ME to go out with someone who looks like you!

She has a face that
could launch a
thousand ships.

* * *

*And it looks like
it has.*

Behind every good man
is a great woman.

* * *

*I read somewhere
saying crap like that
will get me laid.*

Of course I'll respect
you in the morning.

* * *

*Providing you'll be
gone by then.*

It won't hurt.
I promise.

* * *

It will hurt.
And I don't care.

I want to tie you
to the bed.

* * *

Most women run
when they see
me naked.

I'm a real
animal lover.

* * *

*Ever do it
doggie style?*

I PROMISE
I'll pull out
before I...

* * *

...ooops!

Baby, you're the best
I've ever had.

* * *

This week.

I'll call you in the morning.

* * *

I'll call you when they sell snow tires in Hell.

Actually, I prefer oral sex.

* * *

That's because my tongue is longer than my schlong.

HER LIES ...

What She Says

* * *

What She REALLY Means!

I'm a perfect
size 8.

* * *

*But I can breathe
in a 12.*

I'm so tired of the
bar scene.

* * *

*But that's the only
place dark enough
to hide my wrinkles.*

Don't talk.
Just kiss me.

* * *

The sooner we get this over with, the sooner I can watch my Soap.

I didn't know love would be like this.

* * *

Boring, stupid, pathetic...

You're my
BEST friend.

* * *

*Even my dog
won't lick me.*

Who, HIM? He doesn't mean anything to me!

$$* * *$$

Well, if you leave out the great sex.

I could talk with
you for hours.

* * *

*Because you can only
screw for seconds.*

I've always been
a blonde.

* * *

From the waist up,
that is.

Let's try being
"friends" first.

* * *

But SEX????
NEVER IN A
MILLION YEARS!!!!

Do you believe in love
at first sight?

* * *

*Then introduce me to
your friend.*

You're the best looking guy in the bar...

* * *

You're the ONLY guy left and it's closing time.

The way to a man's heart is through his stomach.

* * *

After working your way up from his penis, that is.

Darling, we've shared so much together.

* * *

And in 9 months, we're going to be sharing child support.

I'm only 29...

* * *

...*pounds overweight.*

You're a wonderful dancer.

* * *

For a second, I thought you might be having a seizure.

I'm 38 - 24 - 36.

* * *

Just not in that order.

I'd NEVER have
guessed you wear
a toupee.

* * *

*I thought it was
a Chia Pet.*

No, I can't see your
bald spot at all...

* * *

*Because the glare
is blinding me!*

You're in insurance?
That's fascinating...

* * *

*I've had more
fun talking to
potted plants.*

No, there's no one else in my life right now.

* * *

I couldn't get another date on such short notice.

It's getting late,
you'd better go.

* * *

*My REAL date will be
here in a half-hour.*

I never have sex on the
FIRST date.

* * *

*Maybe that's why
I've never had a
SECOND date.*

I'm already involved in
an intimate relationship.

* * *

*And the best part is,
my vibrator never
lies to me.*

You don't look like you've gained any weight recently.

* * *

You've ALWAYS looked like a walrus.

Don't worry,
I'm on the pill.

* * *

Does aspirin count?

Baby,
you make me wet.

* * *

*Would you quit
drooling?*

Size doesn't matter.

* * *

Unless you're having sex.

Don't worry about impotence honey. It's never happened TWICE to any man I've ever been with.

* * *

Because after the FIRST time, I never saw the wimp again.

No, really,
I like your beard.

* * *

*Just like I enjoy having
my face scraped with
steel wool.*

Darling, you were
made for me...

* * *

...out of used parts.

You look exactly like
Tom Cruise.

* * *

*Except for your
zit-face, your greasy
hair and your
skinny chest!*

You're an
UNBELIEVEABLE
lover.

* * *

*I knew you LIED
when you said you
had 8 inches!*

I'll wait for you forever.

* * *

Or until I get a better offer.

Why don't you let
ME call YOU!

* * *

*I'll call you when pigs
grow wings and fly.*

Can't we just talk
for a while?

* * *

*I'd rather make love
to a trailer hitch.*

Call me sometime.

* * *

Maybe my answering machine will go out with you.

I'm really into
anal sex.

* * *

*All my dates turn out
to be assholes.*

PICK UP LIES

What We Say When We Don't Want To Go Home Alone...

My wife doesn't understand me...

* * *

I hope you are too dumb to understand me as well as SHE does.

Can I buy you
a drink?

* * *

*You're not good
looking enough to
offer you dinner.*

Wanna go get a
cup of coffee?

* * *

*I want to see what
you look like after
I sober up.*

Haven't we met somewhere before?

* * *

I think I screwed you once, but I'm too drunk to remember your name.

I'd really like to get to "know you".

* * *

Well, maybe...after we've screwed.

I'll bet
you're a virgin!

* * *

*The buck-teeth and
pimples are a dead
giveaway.*

Do you come
here often?

* * *

*If you do,
I need to find a
new place to go.*

God, I think you're
the most beautiful
woman in this bar.

* * *

It's amazing how good
you look after I've had
3 Jack Daniels'.

Oh Baby. I'll give you foreplay for hours.

* * *

Because I can only make love for seconds.

Yeah, I played a little ball back in college.

* * *

...pinball in the Student Union.

If I said you have a beautiful body...

* * *

How long would it take for you to figure out I'm a geek.

So, you're into team sports.

* * *

I hear you've screwed every player in the league.

Baby, I'll make you
see stars.

* * *

*You can turn on Leno
after I've finished.*

I'm hung like
a horse.

* * *

A rocking horse.

I love your earrings.

* * *

Why are you wearing them in your nose?

I'm single.

* * *

That is, if you don't count the wife, four kids, two dogs, one cat and a second mortgage.

No, I REALLY like
your necklace.

* * *

*I thought it was a flea
and tick collar.*

Why, yes,
I AM a doctor.

* * *

*I watched General
Hospital once.*

Darling, I want to show you MY world.

* * *

*Lot 7, Space 8,
Beaver Lick
Trailer Park.*

I've got a whopping
9 inches.

* * *

*Actually, I have
3 inches. You'll have
to use your imagination
for the rest.*

I'm a self-made man. I'm in the restaurant business and I travel frequently.

* * *

I dropped out of high school, I wash dishes for a living and I stay at YMCAs.

Your career sounds
so interesting.
Tell me more.

* * *

*I'd rather watch paint
dry. But, you have
incredible tits...*

...and I have a condo in Vail.

* * *

I live with my mother in Peoria.

Really, I AM a photographer for Playboy.

* * *

I have a drawer full of Polaroid's of women just as gullible as you are.

Well, NORMALLY,
I drive a Corvette
or a Jaguar.

* * *

I'm a valet.

MARRIED LIES

The Lies We Tell in Sickness and in Health...

I'm in the mood
for love...

* * *

*Thank God you're
going out of town
for a week.*

Of COURSE I had
an orgasm!

* * *

*Boy, the ceiling really
needs repainting.*

Your foreplay is
like magic.

* * *

*You always make
my good mood
disappear.*

We're just going to have a quiet weekend for two.

* * *

Nobody in their right mind wants to spend time with us.

Birth control? Well,
with my husband,
I use an I.U.D.

* * *

*He doesn't know,
I Usually Don't.)*

We just need a little
time apart.

* * *

Two or three decades
ought to do it.

It's bad luck to see
the bride on her
wedding day.

* * *

*Because you might
catch her in bed with
your best man.*

Our marriage is an equal partnership.

* * *

I forgot to tell you, we're headed for bankruptcy.

I'm sorry, honey, it was all my fault.

* * *

You were wrong but you're too stupid to know it.

I want to make a
home together.

* * *

*I want to sit on the
couch and watch YOU
rearrange furniture.*

Mother is coming for an extended visit.

* * *

Translation: you don't get any...for MONTHS!

We've grown apart.

* * *

You've grown wider.

I tell my wife everything.

* * *

Now you know why she's divorcing me.

I never keep any secrets
from my husband.

* * *

*Fortunately, I have a
very short term
memory...*

Let's have an open
relationship.

* * *

I want to screw my
secretary. You stay
home.

I love you more today
than yesterday.

* * *

*Your stock portfolio
just went up
ten points.*

But darling, our love doesn't need flowers and candy.

* * *

Damn, I forgot your birthday. Again.

I really enjoyed your mother's visit.

* * *

Especially after she left on her broom.

It's the thought
that counts.

* * *

*Just what I wanted.
ANOTHER Dust-Buster
for my birthday.*

Please, baby, give me one more chance.

* * *

I've only screwed two of your three sisters.

No, I'm not mad at you any more.

* * *

I feel much better after I made your meatloaf with Alpo.

It was all my fault,
Dear.

* * *

*It wasn't my fault, but
I'd like to have sex
again before my 100th
birthday.*

I've got to find myself.

* * *

I'm running off with a stripper.

Love will keep
us together.

* * *

*That, and the fear
of Herpes.*

I'm having my period.

* * *

And as far as you're concerned, the tide is in for the next hundred years.

I think your mole
looks cute.

* * *

*I thought you
had cancer.*

I brought you a hot
little number from
Victoria's Secret.

* * *

*It looked great on
my secretary.*

Dear, I'll be an extra day on my business trip.

* * *

My foursome has a 9:00 a.m. tee time.

We never go to bed
together mad.

* * *

*We've had separate
bedrooms since 1986.*

Who? Her?
We're only friends!

* * *

Until she says "Yes".
Then you're history.

Honey,
you're so smart.

* * *

You can't find the
remote control
without my help.

I'll worship you
forever.

* * *

*Now,
go get me a beer.*

No, REALLY!
I like that dress.

* * *

*Been shopping at
Goodwill again?*

WHAT lipstick on my shirt?

* * *

Jeez, I hope she doesn't look on my UNDERWEAR.

The new wallpaper?
I love it.

* * *

*Thank God. I thought
I was having a
psychedelic flashback.*

We've shared
everything together.

* * *

*Yeast infections,
rashes, crabs, ...*

This dinner looks
wonderful.
What is IT?

* * *

*Honey,
where's the cat?*

Our love has aged
like a bottle of
fine wine.

* * *

*You've kept a cork in
"IT" so long, it's turned
to vinegar.*

You are always
on my mind.

* * *

*That's why I take
Prozak.*

Let's savor these
precious moments
together.

* * *

*Will you hurry up!
My husband will
be home soon.*

...in sickness and in
health, 'til death
do us part.

* * *

*Or until my lawyer
figures out how to
break the prenuptial
agreement.*

TITLES BY CCC PUBLICATIONS

Retail $4.99

30 – DEAL WITH IT!
40 – DEAL WITH IT!
50 – DEAL WITH IT!
60 – DEAL WITH IT!
OVER THE HILL – DEAL WITH IT!
RETIRED – DEAL WITH IT!
"?" book
POSITIVELY PREGNANT
WHY MEN ARE CLUELESS
CAN SEX IMPROVE YOUR GOLF?
THE COMPLETE BOOGER BOOK
FLYING FUNNIES
MARITAL BLISS & OXYMORONS
THE VERY VERY SEXY ADULT DOT-TO-DOT BOOK
THE DEFINITIVE FART BOOK
THE COMPLETE WIMP'S GUIDE TO SEX
THE CAT OWNER'S SHAPE UP MANUAL
PMS CRAZED: TOUCH ME AND I'LL KILL YOU!
RETIRED: LET THE GAMES BEGIN
THE OFFICE FROM HELL
FOOD & SEX
FITNESS FANATICS
YOUNGER MEN ARE BETTER THAN RETIN-A
BUT OSSIFER, IT'S NOT MY FAULT

Retail $4.95

YOU KNOW YOU'RE AN OLD FART WHEN...
1001 WAYS TO PROCRASTINATE
HORMONES FROM HELL II
SHARING THE ROAD WITH IDIOTS
THE GREATEST ANSWERING MACHINE MESSAGES OF ALL TIME
WHAT DO WE DO NOW?? (A Guide For New Parents)
HOW TO TALK YOU WAY OUT OF A TRAFFIC TICKET
THE BOTTOM HALF (How To Spot Incompetent Professionals)
LIFE'S MOST EMBARRASSING MOMENTS
HOW TO ENTERTAIN PEOPLE YOU HATE
YOUR GUIDE TO CORPORATE SURVIVAL
THE SUPERIOR PERSON'S GUIDE TO EVERYDAY IRRITATIONS
GIFTING RIGHT

Retail $5.95

THE BOOK OF WHITE TRASH
THE ART OF MOONING
GOLFAHOLICS
WHY GOD MAKES BALD GUYS
LOVE DAT CAT
CRINKLED 'N' WRINKLED
SMART COMEBACKS FOR STUPID QUESTIONS
YIKES! IT'S ANOTHER BIRTHDAY
SEX IS A GAME

SEX AND YOUR STARS
SIGNS YOUR SEX LIFE IS DEAD
40 AND HOLDING YOUR OWN
50 AND HOLDING YOUR OWN
MALE BASHING: WOMEN'S FAVORITE PASTIME
THINGS YOU CAN DO WITH A USELESS MAN
<u>MORE</u> THINGS YOU CAN DO WITH A USELESS MAN
THE WORLD'S GREATEST PUT-DOWN LINES
LITTLE INSTRUCTION BOOK OF THE RICH & FAMOUS
WELCOME TO YOUR MIDLIFE CRISIS
GETTING EVEN WITH THE ANSWERING MACHINE
ARE YOU A SPORTS NUT?
MEN ARE PIGS / WOMEN ARE BITCHES
THE BETTER HALF
ARE WE DYSFUNCTIONAL YET?
TECHNOLOGY BYTES!
50 WAYS TO HUSTLE YOUR FRIENDS ($5.99)
HORMONES FROM HELL
HUSBANDS FROM HELL
KILLER BRAS & Other Hazards Of The 50's
IT'S BETTER TO BE OVER THE HILL THAN UNDER IT
HOW TO REALLY PARTY!!!
WORK SUCKS!
THE PEOPLE WATCHER'S FIELD GUIDE
THE UNOFFICIAL WOMEN'S DIVORCE GUIDE
THE ABSOLUTE LAST CHANCE DIET BOOK
FOR MEN ONLY (How To Survive Marriage)
THE UGLY TRUTH ABOUT MEN
NEVER A DULL CARD
THE LITTLE BOOK OF ROMANTIC LIES
THE LITTLE BOOK OF CORPORATE LIES ($6.95)
RED HOT MONOGAMY (In Just 60 Seconds A Day) ($6.95)
HOW TO SURVIVE A JEWISH MOTHER ($6.95)
WHY MEN DON'T HAVE A CLUE ($7.99)
LADIES, START YOUR ENGINES! ($7.99)

Retail $3.95
NO HANG-UPS
NO HANG-UPS II
NO HANG-UPS III
HOW TO SUCCEED IN SINGLES BARS
HOW TO GET EVEN WITH YOUR EXES
TOTALLY OUTRAGEOUS BUMPER-SNICKERS ($2.95)

NO HANG-UPS – CASSETTES Retail $4.98

Vol. I:	GENERAL MESSAGES (Female)
Vol. I:	GENERAL MESSAGES (Male)
Vol. II:	BUSINESS MESSAGES (Female)
Vol. II:	BUSINESS MESSAGES (Male)
Vol. III:	'R' RATED MESSAGES (Female)
Vol. III:	'R' RATED MESSAGES (Male)
Vol. IV:	SOUND EFFECTS ONLY
Vol. V:	CELEBRI-TEASE